DIRTY LITTLE HOUSE WIFE
Adult Coloring Book

Illustrated By
Cheri Lyn Shull
www.cherishull.com

Special thank you to Lina Weikel for coloring the cover of this book.

All rights reserved. Personal use only.
NO REDISTRUBUTION.

www.cherishull.com

0

www.cherishull.com

Always in the mood to make you CUM

www.cherishull.com

The kind of **DIRTY** You Can't **WASH OFF**

www.cherishull.com

www.cherishull.com

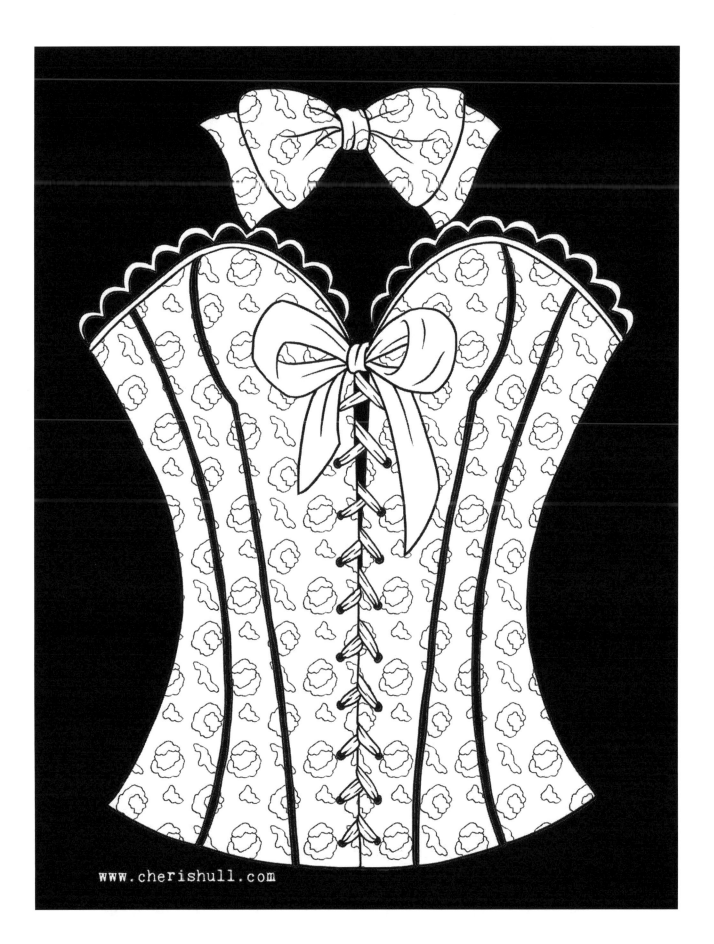

Come hang out with the Queens of Coloring!!

#QueenSassy #QueenSexy #QueenNaughty

www.facebook.com/groups/queensofcoloring

Post colored pages, snag exclusive freebies, play games, hang out with coloring friends, enter coloring contests and lots, lots more!

Must be 18 years or older to join due to mature content.

MORE BOOKS BY ME

Details on where to buy them in the back

YOU MAY ALSO LIKE BOOKS BY Jamesa Lynn Leyhe

Cristin April Frey

Details on where to buy them in the back

Where to Find Cheri Lyn Shull

Books On Amazon

Karleigh Sue
Karleigh Sue's Little Black Book
Karleigh Sue Doodle Therapy
Mary Jane's Adult Coloring Book
www.CheriShull.com

Where to Find Jamesa Lynn Leyhe

Books On Amazon

Naughty Sex Words & Phrases
Fuck My Day
Mommy's Time-Out Swear Words Edition

Join in on the fun at
www.facebook.com/groups/TimeOut.Coloring.Books
www.Time-Out-Adult-Coloring-Books.com

Where to Find Cristin April Frey

Books On Amazon

The Art of Not Giving a Fuck
Sassy Sayings, Snarky Sarcasms & Saucy Swears

Join in on the fun at
www.facebook.com/CristinAprilsArt
www.cristinapril.com

Made in the USA
Lexington, KY
04 November 2016